Cut and Run

A play

Peter Horsler

Samuel French — London
New York - Toronto - Hollywood

CHARACTERS

Super-fit Ted
Marlene, Ted's very unfit wife
Dr Glow
Nurse Bountiful, in love with Dr Glow
Dr Boxclever, a private doctor in the employ of Dupo
Mrs Spout, an NHS patient of the "I know my rights" type
Miss Rosebud, an innocent with whom Dr Glow falls in
    love
Mrs Grimley-Cloned, a wealthy hypochondriac
Mr Widdell, an NHS administrator

The action of the play takes place in a doctor's surgery in
an NHS clinic

Time—the present

COPYRIGHT INFORMATION

(See also page ii)

SYNOPSIS OF SCENES

ACT I

SCENE 1   An NHS clinic

SCENE 2   The same. A month later

ACT II

SCENE 1   The same. Two months later

SCENE 2   The same. The action is continuous

ACT I

Scene 1

An NHS clinic

The composite set is comprised of the end of the waiting-room, the surgery and a small dispensary. A door DR *leads into the waiting-room area where three chairs are set. There are pamphlets on "Looking after your heart" in the waiting-room. The* US *wall in the surgery area, which occupies at least two thirds of the available acting space, has a large bay window looking out on to a brick wall. In the* L *wall of the surgery area are two doors, the* US *one leading into Dr Glow's private flat and the* DS *one leading into the dispensary which is very small but has a table, shelving and floor space for a stool. In the main area there is an examination couch set up in the bay window which has a removable tatty screen around it. Dr Glow's plastic-topped desk is set* LC *facing the audience, with two cheap plastic chairs, one set in front of the desk angled towards the audience and the other behind it. There is a filing cabinet with a top practical drawer, set* DL *on the* L *wall*

The Lights come up on the empty waiting-room area

Marlene enters, calling back to the unseen Ted as she does so

Marlene There's some seats here, Ted. (*She sits on the chair* DS)

   Ted enters, wearing a track suit

Ted immediately does several press-ups, followed by flexing the muscles of both arms. He then picks up a pamphlet on "Looking after your heart" and sits, reading the pamphlet. There is general commotion from the off-stage part of the waiting-room and Mrs Spout's voice is heard

Mrs Spout (*off*) I don't care how long you've been waiting, pregnant women come first! Mind yer legs! Here, move that bag can't yer, before I falls over it!

Mrs Spout, heavily pregnant, appears, and stands in front of Ted

Excuse me!

Ted moves to the R chair to allow her to sit on the L

Phew! Shan't half be pleased when this one's here. (*To Ted*) See what a trouble you men cause. Oughter be ashamed you did. This is my fifth and it don't get no easier.

Marlene Not my Ted's fault, is it? We've never had a family. He's too busy keeping fit.

Ted (*looking up*) Here, listen to this. (*Reading*) "I always thought my husband very healthy and then one day he went out to mow the lawn and dropped dead".

Mrs Spout That's typical that is. Just like a man to drop dead before he cut it.

Marlene Well, we can see you don't let the grass grow under your feet.

Ted You never know, do yer? It says here: (*reading*) "Four out of ten men in Britain will suffer from heart disease before they are sixty-five".

Mrs Spout And what about women? Call that sexual equality?

Marlene No good worrying, Ted. What will be, will be. (*To Mrs Spout*) No good looking for trouble, is it?

Ted I'm trying to prevent it. Not like you with your forty fags a day, buttered toast and fat bacon.

Mrs Grimly-Cloned enters the waiting-room area

Mrs Grimley-Cloned Oh, the pain! The pain! Help me to the doctor!

Mrs Spout You wait yer turn, like the rest of us.

Ted rises and helps Mrs Grimley-Cloned to sit in his place

Mrs Grimley-Cloned (*recovering*) I'll have you know, my good woman, that I have an appointment with Dr Boxclever at 9 a.m.

Mrs Spout Best get a move on then 'cause you're at the wrong place. This here's Dr Glow's clinic.

Mrs Grimley-Cloned I am a member of Dupo!

Mrs Spout What's that then when it's at home?

Marlene It's private health.

Mrs Spout Private, is it? Well, this here's a National Health clinic and don't cater for no snobby, private patients.

Mrs Grimley-Cloned I'll have you know, my good woman, that this is the address I was given. I do not make mistakes.

The Lights cross-fade to the surgery

Dr Glow enters UL, followed by Dr Boxclever, carrying a briefcase,

*containing a stethoscope, a diary and a menu and a very large sports bag,
containing two pictures, a feather duster, a representative nurse's uniform
and a vase of flowers*

Glow (*marching down to the filing cabinet and pulling out files from a
drawer*) Well, all I can say is that nobody has bothered to inform me!
Boxclever (*crossing* R *above the desk*) But you know how it is in these
bureaucracies, my dear chap: news travels slowly.
Glow Not even a phone call.
Boxclever I expect you'll have a sheaf of forms by this morning's post.
Glow (*turning to him*) And in the meantime, I just have to take your word
for it, I suppose.
Boxclever (*taking an envelope from his pocket*) I have a copy of the contract,
if you want to see it. It states quite clearly that the NHS has hired the Clinic
to Dupo from 9 a.m.
Glow Until when?
Boxclever Until I have finished. But don't worry. I rarely have more than
one client—er, patient—at such an early hour and I never spend too long
with them. One has to give the impression that every second is precious.
And of course, at our prices, it is.
Glow (*crossing below him to* LC, *indicating the waiting-room*) I have patients
out there, waiting.
Boxclever Yes, yes, but they're used to that, surely.
Glow And what about Nurse Bountiful? She'll be here any minute.

Nurse Bountiful enters through the waiting-room to Glow's R

Boxclever We've hired her too.
Glow (*to Bountiful as she enters*) Did you know you'd been hired by Dupo?
Bountiful Hired, Dr Glow? You make me sound like Lucy Bedfellow in
Woman For Hire.
Glow From nine until ... oh, this is Dr Boxclever whom you'll be working
for.
Bountiful But I work for you, Doctor. I love working for you. I love——
Boxclever (*offering his hand and eyeing her up and down*) I'm sure we'll
make a great team.
Glow It's only for a few minutes.
Bountiful Oh, well, if you wish it——
Boxclever (*taking charge and crossing below them to the door* L) Now, I've
taken the liberty. Hope you don't mind, old man, but, well, I couldn't ...
not that desk. (*He claps his hands*)

*Three workmen enter, marching to music. The first carries a small set of
steps, the second and third, a pair of curtains already fixed to a curtain pole*

Glow retreats before them to the chair behind the desk, Bountiful to the other chair. The first workman pulls the couch forward and sets the steps before the window

The first workman then moves down, tips Bountiful out of the chair and carries it off

Bountiful flees into the dispensary, as the second and third workmen set the curtains

The third workman now removes Glow's desk

Glow exits UL *in disgust*

The second workman removes Glow's chair and carries that off

The first workman enters with an antique carver chair which he sets as the new desk chair

The second and third workmen enter with an antique desk which they set where the plastic desk had been

(*To the workmen, pointing at the screens*) And don't forget those disgusting screens. (*During the following, he replaces the two medical charts with two gold-framed pictures*)

The first workman exits

The second and third workmen carry off the old screen

The first workman enters with a new-looking, folding screen. He sets it R *of the window. He then moves the couch back into position and takes the steps off*

Boxclever takes a small vase of flowers from his bag and places it on the desk. He places his bag on the desk, takes out a few brochures and documents which we cannot see and then tries out the comfortable, padded chair

Nurse Bountiful enters from the dispensary, now wearing a plain white coat. She moves to above the desk

Oh dear, no, Nurse. I don't think that will do at all. (*He dives into his bag and pulls out a smart white costume with a split skirt and a chic little nurse's cap with "Dupo" embroidered on it*) Here, put this on. When you work for me, I expect your dress to suit our image.

Bountiful Image, Doctor?

Boxclever Yes, first impressions, Nurse, are all important. You are part of the total package, like the dust cover on a novel.

Bountiful I read a great deal, Doctor, and I know that cover pictures rarely relate to what's in the book.

Boxclever Quite so, but that's not important. It's selling them that matters.

Bountiful (*taking the costume*) I only do this because Dr Glow asked me to. I do not view it as the role of a heroine.

Nurse Bountiful accepts the proffered garments and goes off UL to change

The Lights cross-fade to the waiting-room

Ted (*to Mrs Grimley-Cloned*) I bet you're here because of your angina.

Mrs Grimley-Cloned I beg your pardon?

Ted Angina.

Mrs Grimley-Cloned How dare you!

Ted Sorry. Your heart's all right then?

Mrs Grimley-Cloned My heart?

Ted Angina's a heart condition.

Mrs Grimley-Cloned Oh. What I am here for, my good man, is my business. I do not wish to discuss my health in public.

Marlene Take no notice. Ted's become a real hypochondriac since he gave up work. Winning the Pools was the worst thing that could have happened for him. Now it's all keep fit and no fun.

Ted (*to Marlene*) You'll be sorry one day. All that chocolate and cream doughnuts and your smoking——

Marlene "Little bit of what yer fancy", is what I say.

Mrs Spout What I say an' all.

They all turn to stare at her. The Lights come up on the surgery area

Nurse Bountiful enters UL

Bountiful It's nine o'clock, Dr Boxclever.

Boxclever That's better, Nurse. Pity our only patient this morning is female. Still, I appreciate the new packaging. (*He consults a file*) Now would you see if Mrs Grimley-Cloned has arrived.

Nurse Bountiful crosses to the waiting-room

Ted You don't have to die young, you know, you do have a choice.

Bountiful looks round

Bountiful (*to Mrs Grimley-Cloned*) Mrs Grimley-Cloned?
Mrs Grimley-Cloned (*rising*) That is I.
Bountiful Dr Boxclever will see you now.

Mrs Grimley-Cloned follows Nurse Bountiful into the surgery area

Mrs Spout She wants to see a private doctor, she shouldn't come to a public clinic. She should go to Harvey Street.

The Lights fade down on the waiting-room area. Dr Boxclever rises to greet Mrs Grimley-Cloned

Boxclever My dear Mrs Grimley-Cloned. (*He helps her into the chair in front of the desk*) And how are we today?
Mrs Grimley-Cloned Oh, Doctor, if only you knew——
Boxclever (*massaging her neck*) But I do, good lady, I do.
Mrs Grimley-Cloned The agony.
Boxclever I know. Such fortitude. You put such a brave face on it.
Mrs Grimley-Cloned Shall I ever be cured, Doctor?
Boxclever Not if I can help it—I mean—with my help, dear lady, with my help. But has there been no improvement?
Mrs Grimley-Cloned I'm afraid not, Doctor. The hippopotamus oil brought me out in hives.
Boxclever Dear, dear.
Mrs Grimley-Cloned And I just couldn't take the monkey-gland extract. I found the thought quite nauseating.
Boxclever I'm not surprised, dear lady, not in the least. The more refined and sensitive of my patients usually have this problem. I wonder if a further examination might reveal——
Mrs Grimley-Cloned Please, Doctor, please.
Boxclever Nurse, would you warm the couch for Mrs Grimley-Cloned.
Bountiful Warm it, Doctor?
Boxclever Yes, of course, do you think I can run the risk of Mrs Grimley-Cloned getting a chill? She is in a very delicate state, you know.
Bountiful But how shall I warm it, Doctor?
Boxclever Lie on it, woman.
Bountiful Yes, Doctor. (*She goes* US *and removes the screens to reveal the examination couch. She then climbs on it and lies down*)

Boxclever helps Mrs Grimley-Cloned, who seems to have lost all use of her legs, up to the couch

Boxclever Gently, dear lady, gently does it.

Mrs Grimley-Cloned Oh, oh, Doctor, the pain, the agony! I can't begin to tell you——

Boxclever Of course you can't, dear lady, of course you can't. Lean on me. (*To Nurse Bountiful*) Is that couch warm yet, Nurse?

Bountiful I'm doing my best, Doctor.

Boxclever Well, radiate, Nurse, radiate! We haven't got all day.

Mrs Grimley-Cloned (*putting her arms round Boxclever's neck*) Oh, hold me, Doctor, I think I'm going to faint.

Boxclever (*struggling to escape from Mrs Grimley-Cloned's embraces*) Well, help me to get her on the couch, Nurse!

They lift Mrs Grimley-Cloned on to the couch

Mrs Grimley-Cloned Oh, ooh, eeh, it's agony!

Boxclever Thank you, Nurse, that will be all for the present. I'll call you if I need you.

Boxclever ushers Bountiful into the dispensary, patting her on the bottom as she exits

Very radiant, a great asset. (*He consults his diary on the desk*) Now let me see. Ah yes, we've tried the cider baths.

Mrs Grimley-Cloned Gave me hiccups, Doctor.

Boxclever And the newt's tongue soup.

Mrs Grimley-Cloned I just couldn't drink it, Doctor. I don't know why.

Boxclever All part of your condition, dear lady. But we haven't tried the "all over feather tickle", have we? (*He takes a feather duster from his bag*)

Mrs Grimley-Cloned That sounds promising, Doctor.

Boxclever moves over to her, draws the screens around the couch and disappears behind, waving the feather duster

Ooh, ooh, eeh, ooh! I feel better already.

Boxclever Stimulates the tactile corpuscles and the capillary vessels.

Mrs Grimley-Cloned Yes, yes.

Boxclever So good for the epidermis.

Mrs Grimley-Cloned Oh, yes, yes.

Boxclever (*coming from behind the screen*) Well, that's all for the moment. (*He moves to the desk*) Do you want to pay now or shall I put it on your account? (*He sits*)

Mrs Grimley-Cloned (*emerging from behind the screen*) I feel so much better, Doctor. (*She sits on the chair in front of the desk*) Do you think I can ever be completely cured?

Boxclever I only wish I could be more reassuring, dear lady, but your condition is extremely rare. Not much is known about it except that it appears to attack those with breeding and money. I can't afford to promise you a complete cure; it wouldn't be ethical.

Mrs Grimley-Cloned Then I am condemned to a life of agony. Is that what you are trying to tell me?

Boxclever I shall always be here to relieve you of your wealth—health problems. Though I did hear——

Mrs Grimley-Cloned Yes, yes?

Boxclever No, it's out of the question. Impossibly expensive.

Mrs Grimley-Cloned (*sitting up quickly*) Tell me, tell me!

Boxclever The Japanese have discovered a cure but as yet not on a commercial basis. The process to produce this elixir takes hundreds of man hours and vast resources. I have a friend—no, no, that would not be ethical.

Mrs Grimley-Cloned (*jumping up*) To hell with your ethics!

Boxclever Well, just for you, I might get some smuggled here in the diplomatic bag but it would cost a small fortune.

Mrs Grimley-Cloned (*thumping the desk*) I must have it! I need it!

Boxclever Very well. If you could write me a cheque for five thousand pounds, I'll do what I can.

Mrs Grimley-Cloned (*sitting*) Dear, dear, Dr Boxclever.

Boxclever Yes, I am, aren't I?

Mrs Grimley-Cloned Of course, I shall have to economise. Give up some of my little pleasures. No more hampers from Fortnums; cancel my next *Canberra* cruise. I haven't won the Pools, you know, like that wretched man out there in the waiting-room. Oh, but it will be worth it. Just fancy, I could know what it is to feel well again.

Boxclever What wretched man?

Mrs Grimley-Cloned Oh, a frightful type in a track suit. Hardly the sort you'd want in Dupo, I should think.

Boxclever Oh, I don't know.

Mrs Grimley-Cloned What?

Boxclever I don't know what the world is coming to.

Mrs Grimley-Cloned Quite. Now, your cheque. (*She collects her handbag from the chair*) Shall I make it out to Dupo?

Boxclever No, no. I'm afraid they might not approve of diplomatic bags etc. Better to make it out to me.

Mrs Grimley-Cloned You dear, dear, naughty man.

Boxclever I'll get Nurse Bountiful to ring the Japanese Embassy.

Boxclever goes into the dispensary, the Lights coming up on that area as he does so. Mrs Grimley-Cloned writes her cheque on the doctor's table

Nurse Bountiful, could you ring Benson's Garage for me to see if they've finished my car.

Bountiful Of course, Doctor.

Boxclever ushers Bountiful through the surgery to the door UL *and then returns to Mrs Grimley-Cloned*

Boxclever She's gone to ring the Japanese Embassy to try to contact my friend. (*He takes the cheque from her and examines it*) It gives me great pleasure to relieve you of this—to bring you relief.
Mrs Grimley-Cloned Dear Dr Boxclever, where would I be without you?
Boxclever Where indeed.
Mrs Grimley-Cloned My life would be so much poorer.
Boxclever Oh, I doubt that, dear lady. (*He ushers her towards the waiting-room*) But of course you can rely on me to find alternative treatments for you. We can always resort to surgery if necessary. Sir Francis Prune is highly skilled. He gives an excellent cut. I mean, there would be no scars to speak of.

The Lights cross-fade to the waiting-room area as they move there

Boxclever accompanies Mrs Grimley-Cloned to the waiting-room door DR, *watches her go with the door open and then addresses Ted*

You weren't waiting to see me, were you?
Ted No. Dr Glow.
Boxclever I could fit you in as it happens—as I've had a cancellation.
Ted Better stick to my doctor.
Boxclever It would be quite free and without obligation. A second opinion is always worthwhile, you know.
Marlene He hasn't had a first opinion yet.
Boxclever No matter, dear lady. The order is not important.
Mrs Spout That's where you're wrong. He's not goin' in before us. Queue jumpin'!
Boxclever This would be a private matter.
Mrs Spout Thought you said it was free.
Boxclever Oh, yes, quite free but we reserve the right to treat only those patients that we choose to.
Mrs Spout And just what are you gettin' at? I suppose I'm not good enough for yer?
Marlene Why don't you, Ted? Can't do any harm. If two doctors tell you you're quite fit, perhaps you'll believe them.
Mrs Spout (*to Boxclever*) Here, I asked you a question!
Boxclever (*to Mrs Spout*) A rhetorical one, surely.
Mrs Spout A what?

Ted Will Dr Glow mind?

Marlene You haven't seen him yet, so you're not his patient and this Dr——

Boxclever Boxclever.

Marlene Dr Boxclever don't mind you seein' him afterwards.

Boxclever Not at all.

Mrs Spout What do yer mean by "historical"?

Marlene Go on, Ted.

Ted Oh, all right then.

Boxclever This way. (*He moves to his desk*)

Ted follows Boxclever

The Lights cross-fade to the surgery area

Mrs Spout (*after them*) Here, I asked yer——

Boxclever Do sit down, my good fellow. (*He sits behind his desk*)

Ted sits in the chair in front of it

Now, what appears to be the trouble?

Ted Nothing I can put my finger on, Doctor. I don't just feel quite right.

Boxclever So you'd like a general check-over.

Ted Well, yes.

Boxclever Of course, under normal circumstances, I should at this point ask which option you prefer. We do two check-overs, standard and deluxe. Basically, the standard means looking at the outside bits, and the deluxe outside and inside—as far as possible that is. (*He rises and takes his stethoscope from his bag on the table*) But of course, this is just a free sample to put your mind at rest. (*He moves to Ted's R*) Open your mouth. (*He peers down Ted's throat*) Oh, dear. (*He looks in his eyes*) Oh, dear, oh dear. (*He feels his pulse*) Oh, my goodness.

Ted Something wrong, Doctor?

Boxclever My dear fellow. I have to tell you that you are very seriously ill indeed. Immediate surgery is your only hope.

Ted Why, what have I got?

Boxclever What have you not. Aren't you in pain?

Ted Only from my bunion and I've had that for years.

Boxclever Ah, that could be the root of the infection. It's travelling up from your foot.

Ted What is?

Boxclever One of the nastiest little viruses known to man.

Ted Oh dear.

Boxclever I'll have to get you into hospital at once. I'm afraid it will cost you rather a lot but it's your only hope.

Ted (*struggling to rise*) I should see Dr Glow.

Boxclever (*pushing him down*) No time.

Ted But if he thinks it's urgent, he'll——

Boxclever By the time he's cut through the red tape, you'll need an undertaker not a surgeon.

Ted Well, you know best, Doctor. Will I need surgery then?

Boxclever Undoubtedly.

Ted They'll cut the bunion out?

Boxclever That would be too cheap and easy. We don't want any botched jobs, do we? If a garden shed's rotten, pull it down and start again, that's what I say.

Ted (*rising and moving to him*) Pull it down?

Boxclever Or in your case, cut it off.

Ted What, my foot?

Boxclever No, no, my dear chap, your leg.

Ted My leg?

Boxclever Must be thorough, mustn't we?

Ted Yes, but the leg's all right. I mean I can run and——

Boxclever Ah yes, but that's today. We have to think of tomorrow. Bunions usually prove fatal unless they are treated quite drastically.

Ted I know you know best, Doctor, but wouldn't they consider just part of the foot?

Boxclever shakes his head

Well, just the foot then?

Boxclever shakes his head again

Just below the knee?

Boxclever Possibly, if we can get Prune, but if we have to use Hacker it will be all or nothing.

Ted Hacker?

Boxclever A fine surgeon but a little OTT. Likes to work on a large canvas if you follow me?

Ted (*backing away from him and sinking on the chair*) I fear I do. Try to get Mr Prune, please.

Boxclever He is more expensive. Slower, you see, because of his meticulous attention to detail. But in my opinion worth every extra penny.

Ted Well, you know best, Doctor.

Boxclever Of course, I do. I'll ring for an ambulance. (*He helps Ted up*) I'll help you through to Dr Glow's lounge. (*He takes a paper from his desk and hands it to Ted*) Perhaps you'd like to look at this week's menu while you're waiting. We have a new chef, straight from the Ritz, I believe. Now that you've decided to go private, every luxury shall be yours.

Nurse Bountiful enters UL *and crosses to above* R *of the desk*

Bountiful Doctor, the garage doesn't seem to know anything about your car.
Boxclever (*escorting Ted to the door* UL) Never mind that, Nurse, I have to attend to my patient's needs. You can tell Glow that he may as well use my desk from now on.
Ted What about my wife?
Boxclever I'll see she's informed.

Mrs Spout bursts in

During the following, Marlene moves into the position next to the door

I think Dr Glow has his first patient. Must fly.

Boxclever and Ted exit

Mrs Spout And what time do yer call this? (*To Bountiful*) Where the 'eck's Dr Glow?
Bountiful (*crossing to her*) Surgery will start any minute. Would you kindly wait outside until Dr Glow sends for you?
Mrs Spout And where do yer think I've been waiting? And waiting. I'm fed up with waiting. Private patients in a National Health clinic—it ain't right!

Dr Glow enters UL

Bountiful It's no good you complaining to us. See your local MP.
Glow Why is the telephone off the hook, Nurse? Ah, Mrs Spout. Why is she here?
Bountiful She just burst in, Doctor.
Glow Did she. Has she an appointment?
Mrs Spout Yes, I has.
Bountiful (*crossing to the filing cabinet*) Well, that's easily checked.
Glow Even so, Mrs Spout. We can't have you bursting in. You must wait until Nurse calls you.
Mrs Spout Oh yes, it's all right for the likes of me ter wait, ain't it? I ain't got a la-di-dah voice and don't slip yer a backhander——
Bountiful How dare you suggest that dear Dr Glow can be bribed?

Mrs Spout Everyone has their price, ducky. If you ain't learnt that you ain't learned nothing.

Bountiful (*crossing to her* R) You ungrateful woman! Don't you know that Dr Glow puts his patients before his own health. He is a missionary, every bit as brave as Julian Threadgold in *Dark Souls in Torment*.

Mrs Spout Who?

Glow An entirely fictional character. Now, Mrs Spout, if you'll kindly return to the waiting-room, I will consult my list to see if you come next.

Mrs Spout You do that. I'll wait here.

Glow No, Mrs Spout. If you do not return to the waiting-room, I shall abandon surgery.

Mrs Spout Here, you can't do that!

Glow (*pointing dramatically*) To the waiting-room, Mrs Spout!

Mrs Spout (*crumbling*) I pay me rates and me taxes. (*She crosses to the waiting-room*) I've got me rights. Doctors should have more respect.

The Lights come up on the waiting-room as Mrs Spout goes there

Bountiful exits UL

(*To Marlene*) Here, you're in my place, move over!

Marlene Sorry, thought you'd gone in.

Mrs Spout He ain't ready. Move over!

Rosebud enters and crosses behind Mrs Spout

As Marlene slides across, Rosebud sits in her place

What the...? Where'd you come from?

Rosebud Pardon?

Mrs Spout You're in my place!

Marlene moves R *so that Rosebud can make room for Mrs Spout who after glaring at Rosebud, sits*

I should think so an' all. No bloody manners these days, that's the trouble.

The Lights fade down on the waiting-room

Bountiful enters UL *now dressed in the drab, white coat*

Bountiful Oh, Dr Glow, you were so masterful. How I wish our relationship could be more than the professional.

Glow I am wedded to Medicine, Nurse, you know that. If there was room
in my heart for more, I'm sure you would be the tenant.
Bountiful Oh, Doctor. Would that be the right ventricle or the left?
Glow Which ever takes your fancy. (*He becomes very professional*) Now,
Nurse, would you mind showing Mrs Spout in.
Bountiful (*with adoring eyes*) Yes, Doctor. Of course, Doctor. (*She goes
into the waiting-room*)

Glow busies himself with reading notes

Er—next please.
Mrs Spout 'Bout time an' all.

*Mrs Spout follows Bountiful through into the surgery and sits herself in the
chair facing Glow*

Glow (*opening a file*) All coming along nicely, Mrs Spout, is it?
Mrs Spout I dunno, do I? You're the doctor. Ain't you goin' ter take me
blood pressure then?
Glow Nurse will do that. If you come to the pre-natal clinic, Friday mornings,
we can keep a check on everything for you.
Mrs Spout No, I can't come on a Friday morning. I does me shoppin' then.
I wants a check-over now.
Glow Not having any problems, are you?
Mrs Spout No more than usual.
Glow Not feeling excessively tired?
Mrs Spout No more than usual.
Glow Well then, I'm sure everything's fine. Just give me a call if you're
worried about something and do try to come to the clinic.
Mrs Spout Is that it then? Don't I get no vitamins or nothing?
Glow Come to the clinic.
Mrs Spout (*rising*) Huh, fine doctor you is! Don't get nothing these days.
If yer poor that is! (*She moves to the waiting-room door*) Right, I shall be
writin' to the chief doctor. Then you'd better watch out!

Mrs Spout exits DR

Glow Who's next, Nurse?

*Bountiful goes into the waiting-room, the Lights coming up there as she does
so. Glow goes to the filing cabinet and selects a file*

Bountiful Next please.

Marlene (*rising*) That'll be me. Do you know where my husband is, Nurse? He went in to see Dr Boxclever ages ago.

Bountiful You are?

Marlene Mrs Trusting.

Bountiful Ah yes, he went with the Doctor. I expect he'll be back soon. Have you an appointment with Dr Glow?

Marlene Can I use my husband's? I've not been too good lately but what with Ted worryin' himself to death——

Bountiful It's highly irregular but Dr Glow is very understanding. You'd better come in.

Bountiful leads Marlene into the surgery. The Lights fade down on the waiting-room

Doctor, can you see Mrs Trusting instead of Mr Trusting?

Glow (*not looking up from his paper, not really comprehending*) Yes, yes, Nurse, of course, I have the file here. Sit down, please. (*He consults the notes*) Not seen you for some time? That penis trouble cleared up all right?

Marlene Eh?

Glow And the sore scrotum? (*He turns to look at her*) Oh!

Marlene Nurse thought you might see me instead of my husband.

Glow (*moving to sit at his desk*) Indisposed is he?

Marlene He's disappeared.

Glow Well, get him to make another appointment when he turns up. Now, what's your problem?

Marlene Not feeling quite——

Glow Up to the mark?

Marlene Yes.

Glow (*rising and moving to her* R) Let's see then, shall we? Do you smoke?

Marlene Yes.

Glow (*examining her eyes*) What about diet? Eat plenty of fibre? Keep off too much dairy produce? Oh dear... (*He uses his stethoscope*) Let's listen to the old ticker.

Marlene I know I eat too much and shouldn't smoke but——

Glow Nurse, would you get Mrs Trusting on to the couch and take her blood pressure! (*He dives for the phone on his desk*) I must phone for an ambulance at once.

Marlene Is something wrong, Doctor?

Bountiful (*coming to her*) Come along, Mrs Trusting, nothing to worry about. (*She helps her on to the couch*)

Glow (*into the phone*) Ambulance, yes, ambulance! ... Look this is an emergency! ... All right, I'll hold but this is a matter of life and death. ... I said, life and death! ... What? ... Do I mean, "life or death"? I mean if

you don't get your finger out, you'll be responsible for a person's life. ...
All right, all right! I suppose I do mean their "death"!
Marlene (*to Bountiful*) Oh dear, is there an emergency on?
Bountiful Nothing you need be concerned with, Mrs Trusting. Don't worry,
Dr Glow's a wonderful person, I mean, doctor.
Glow (*into the phone*) Dr Glow, the Clinic in Cornerstone Road. ... Of
course you know it; we're one of your outposts. ... I know we're not
officially listed as an outpost! I just used that term—look, get me the Senior
Administrative Officer. ... What? ... Well, anybody who can send an
ambulance at once! ... Is it a priority? ... No, no, I have a woman in my
surgery that could drop dead any second. Would you like me to ring you
when she does? Would that constitute an emergency!
Marlene Oh dear, it does sound as if someone is very ill, doesn't it?
Glow Right, Dr Herman Glow——
Bountiful (*to herself*) Oh, Herman.
Glow The Clinic, Cornerstone Road, Crackenwell. Emergency, imminent
coronary. Does that complete your form?
Marlene Perhaps I should come back when Doctor's not quite so busy.
Bountiful No, no, it's all right, dear, just lie quiet. Have a little rest.
Marlene I do feel tired. Ted's been so demanding since he's thought he was
ill. I do believe I could go to sleep.
Bountiful Well, you do that, dear.
Glow (*into the phone*) Thank you. What a relief it is to us doctors to know
you're there in case of emergencies. ... Yes, I know, it's the cuts. ... Well,
tell them to buy some more ambulances with the money they get from
renting out my clinic! (*To Bountiful*) They'll be here in a few minutes. How
is she?
Bountiful Asleep, Doctor.
Glow Well, keep an eye on her, but I might as well see the next patient.

*Bountiful nods and crosses into the waiting-room, the Lights coming up on
that area as she does so*

Bountiful (*to Rosebud*) Have you an appointment?
Rosebud No, I'm afraid I came on the off chance.
Bountiful I'm sure he'll fit you in. He's so caring, so good, so—er—what
name is it, please?
Rosebud Rosebud.
Bountiful Well, Miss Rosebud, Doctor will see you now.

*Bountiful leads Rosebud into the surgery and then disappears behind the
screen. When Rosebud reaches RC, Dr Glow looks up and their eyes meet.
There is the sound of heavenly voices and the twang of two arrows striking.
They react. It is love at first sight. Bountiful sees what has happened*

(*To the audience over the screen*) It is *Love's Golden Arrow* come to be in real life. (*She covers her face in grief and disappears behind the screen*)

Glow Please, do not ask me to treat you. If I do, my hippocratic oath will prevent us ever having anything more than a doctor/patient relationship (*he moves to her one step at a time*) and this is—this is—for me this is——

Rosebud (*moving towards him*) Oh, and for me.

Glow It is——

Rosebud It is——

Glow ⎫
Rosebud ⎭ (*together, meeting, taking hands*) It is love at first sight!

Nurse Bountiful looks round the screen and registers her distress. She covers her face with her hands and withdraws behind the screen

Glow (*taking Rosebud's hand*) I cannot bear to be so close to you in such sterile surroundings. (*He turns away from her with a dramatic gesture*) Please go now and see another doctor.

Rosebud But I didn't come for myself.

Glow (*turning back*) Ah.

Rosebud It is my poor, old mother. She is so frail that she can no longer run in the London Marathon.

Glow Dear, dear.

Rosebud And this morning she sent her sledgehammer to the car boot sale.

Glow A very bad sign.

Rosebud I fear she is losing the will to live.

Glow I will call round as soon as surgery is over. But you, my dear, are looking tired and strained.

Rosebud What?

Glow Not that it impairs your wondrous beauty. You are like the most fragile orchid.

Rosebud Ah. It is just the financial worry. Mother has spent everything on weight training and now our landlord says he will put us out on the streets unless we pay him a thousand pounds in the next three months.

Glow You poor dear.

Rosebud I cannot work. I daren't leave her in case she tries mixing concrete by hand. Oh, what are we to do? (*She sobs*)

Glow If only I could help but I have reached the limit on all my credit cards and have an overdraft at the bank.

Rosebud No, no, I couldn't let you.

Glow But I can't.

Rosebud Which makes it so much easier for me to refuse.

Glow (*escorting her to the door* DR) Go now. I will call round. I will try to think of something. But please, see another doctor.

Rosebud I will, Doctor. And thank you.
Glow Please call me Herman.
Rosebud Thank you, He man.

They kiss in the subdued light of the waiting-room. As they do so a doorbell rings off L

Nurse Bountiful runs, sobbing, from behind the screen to exit UL

Dr Glow sees Rosebud out of the waiting-room door and then crosses back into the surgery

Glow (*calling*) How is the patient, Nurse? I hope I can rely on your discretion with regard to my encounter with Miss Rosebud. You can bear witness that nothing untoward took place. Nurse? (*He looks behind the screen. To himself as he emerges*) Thank goodness.

Nurse Bountiful enters UL

(*Turning to her*) Ah, there you are, Nurse. Why did you leave our patient?
Bountiful The ambulance has arrived, Doctor, but the men refuse to cross the threshold because the clinic has been used for private practice.
Glow Dear, dear, the patient should always come first. We must be our own stretcher bearers, Nurse.

Dr Glow and Bountiful move the screens and wheel the couch, or use a stretcher from under it, to take Marlene off UL

As soon as they have gone, Widdell enters through the door DR. *He is a ferret of a man, carrying a large briefcase which he thumps down on to Dr Glow's desk and then takes out a notebook which he consults as he looks round the room*

Nurse Bountiful enters

Bountiful (*seeing Widdell*) Oh! Who are——?
Widdell (*taking an identity card from his breast pocket which he holds out to her without looking up*) Widdell.
Bountiful I beg your pardon?
Widdell (*looking at her*) Widdell from Admin.
Bountiful Oh, well——

Dr Glow enters UL

Widdell Just a spot check, you know.

Glow What's this?

Widdell Are you Glow or Boxclever?

Glow I'm Glow, but I don't see——

Widdell (*crossing* R *to* DR) No, well, we move in mysterious ways in Admin. Don't we? To the layman that is. (*He turns back to Glow*) I must say, Glow, that we are not pleased, not in the least. Your phone bills are too high and——

Bountiful (*moving down to Widdell's* L) Mr Widdell, Dr Glow is most economical with the phone. It's this new Dr Boxclever who——

Widdell Now, now, we were not talking to you, Nurse, I think.

Bountiful But it's not fair.

Widdell Nurses should be seen and not heard.

Glow (*moving down to face Widdell*) This is outrageous, Widdell, outrageous!

Widdell Outrageous is it, Glow! Well let me tell you, we think it's outrageous to call an ambulance for minor ailments.

Glow Minor…? What right have you to start making clinical judgements? The patient was in imminent danger of a coronary. She could easily have died because of your administrative delays.

Widdell Ah, but she didn't, which I think rather proves my point.

Boxclever enters UL

(*Crossing up to Boxclever's* R) Ah, you must be Dr Boxclever?

Boxclever Yes. (*To Glow*) A new patient for me?

Widdell No, no, though I'm sure I'd be charmed. No, I'm Widdell, from Admin. But call me James or, like my close friends, Jimmy.

Bountiful (*to herself*) Jimmy Widdell, I don't believe it.

Boxclever (*to Glow*) Just popped in, Glow, to check that phone calls are covered by Dupo's rent.

Widdell But of course, my dear chap, feel free to use it as much as you need.

Boxclever Good. I thought as much. Best to check, though, in case I get charged personally. Have to go easy on the transatlantics then, eh?

Widdell Oh, yes, that wouldn't do at all. (*His face slowly cracks into a grin and then he emits a high-pitched laugh*)

Boxclever (*to Glow*) Just thought I'd check before I try a bit of cold selling.

Boxclever exits UL

Widdell (*going to his case and sitting at Glow's desk*) And I must warn you, Glow, that I have a complete record of all your prescriptions. You've been very liberal with expensive drugs, especially with the elderly.

Glow Naturally, they're the ones who need them most.

Widdell We cannot always be concerned with needs, Glow. We must consider the costs.
Bountiful (*moving to above the desk*) Dr Glow always puts his patients first.
Widdell Exactly my complaint. The service comes first and that means the costs of running it.
Bountiful But I don't understand. What is the Service for if not——
Widdell Quite right, Nurse, such things are beyond your comprehension and none of your business.
Glow (*crossing quickly to Widdell's* L) Now look here, Widdell!
Widdell (*rising*) I advise you not to threaten me, Doctor. He who holds the purse has the power. Now, (*he takes out a huge bundle of forms*) we shall want all these completed by the weekend and in triplicate, if you don't mind. (*He moves to the door* DR) We shall be monitoring you very closely from now on and if you want your precious clinic to survive, I advise you to think very carefully about economizing. Good morning.

Widdell goes

Glow sinks on to his chair

Bountiful What a dreadful man! I hope you will report him.
Glow Who would listen.
Bountiful I would, Doctor. I could listen to you for ever.
Glow You are very loyal, Nurse.
Bountiful More than loyal. I am in——
Glow But we have work to do.
Bountiful (*flatly*) Yes, there's always that.
Glow So you tidy up the dispensary while I fill in a few of these forms before I start my rounds.
Bountiful Yes, Doctor.

Bountiful goes into the dispensary

Dr Glow sits at his desk and wearily draws the pile of forms to him. As he starts on the first one, we hear a kaleidoscope of voices on tape

Mrs Spout's Voice Don't I get no vitamins?
Glow's Voice I have a woman in my surgery who could drop dead any second. Would you like me to ring you when she does? Would that constitute an emergency!
Widdell's Voice I must say, Glow, that we are not pleased, not in the least.
Boxclever's Voice Just thought I'd check.
Mrs Spout's Voice I know me rights. Doctors should have more respect.
Widdell's Voice We must consider the costs.

Nurse Bountiful enters from the dispensary and moves to above the desk. She is now wearing the coat she arrived in

Bountiful I'm off now, Doctor. If you don't mind me saying, I think you should take a holiday. In this week's *Hearts and Flowers* they're advertising a week in Hollywood, two for the price of one.
Glow Yes, thank you, Nurse, but there's too much work, just too much work.
Bountiful (*moving* DR) Ah, well, perhaps next year. I can always hope.

Bountiful exits DR

Boxclever enters UL

Boxclever I say, Glow, old chap. I've just had a thought. If we went into partnership——
Glow (*rising*) No, thank you, Boxclever. No, thank you! All people have the right to the best medical treatment there is, regardless of their means. I shall never treat people for profit, never!
Boxclever (*rather taken back by this outburst*) All right, old chap, all right, I only asked.

Boxclever exits UL

Dr Glow picks up a handful of forms and throws them in the air as the CURTAIN *falls*

SCENE 2

The same, a month later

When the CURTAIN *rises, the Lights come up on the dispensary where Boxclever is seen pouring pink jollop from a gallon jar into a small medicine bottle. He puts the jar away in a cupboard and slips the small bottle into the pocket of his white coat. He then moves into the surgery, the Lights coming up there as he does so. He moves to the desk and consults his diary*

Nurse Bountiful enters DR, *dressed in her outdoor clothes*

Bountiful Good morning, Doctor, am I working for you this morning?
Boxclever You work for me any time, Nurse Bountiful. Why don't you call me Victor when we are alone?
Bountiful Dr Glow wouldn't like it.
Boxclever Dr Glow doesn't seem to want it.

Bountiful He lavishes all his love on his patients.
Boxclever Yes, well, I love my patients. The female ones that is. Those that will let me. Those that I fancy.
Bountiful He is drained of love. There is nothing left for me.
Boxclever It can be very exhausting, I must admit that.

Bountiful goes into the dispensary to take off her coat

Glow enters UL

Ah, Glow, old chap, I'm seeing Mrs Grimley-Cloned this morning and she's asked me for a second opinion. There's a thousand pounds in it for you, if you'd like to——

We hear the heavenly choir sound followed by Rosebud's voice on tape

Rosebud's Voice And now our landlord says he will put us out on to the streets unless we pay him a thousand pounds in the next three months.
Glow A thousand pounds! You did say, "a thousand pounds"?
Boxclever Needn't take you a moment.
Glow (*moving* DRC) If only it were ethical!
Boxclever (*following down to Glow's* L) But of course, my dear chap. No more than those little insurance jobs that come your way from time to time.

Bountiful is about to come back into the surgery after taking her coat off when she stops to hear what Boxclever is saying. She opens the door a crack and listens

Glow I never charge my patients. I could never work for money.
Boxclever The Health Service pays you, doesn't it?
Glow That is a salary.
Boxclever Paid for by the people. So what's the difference?
Glow The difference is that I am free to treat those who need it, not just those that can afford it.
Boxclever But, my dear fellow, if we let those pay who can afford to, it leaves more for those who cannot. Any patient is entitled to a second opinion, are they not?
Glow But of course.
Boxclever But this one can well afford to pay for the service. So let her pay and that leaves you free to see another poor patient.
Glow I don't quite——
Boxclever (*losing patience*) You wouldn't refuse to see a patient?
Glow No, no, of course not.

Boxclever Well, see this one, charge her for it and give the money to some
  charity if you must.

Again we hear Rosebud's voice on tape

Rosebud's Voice He will put us out on to the street unless we pay him a
  thousand pounds.
Glow Very well, a straightforward opinion, no collusion?
Boxclever My dear fellow, are you suggesting——
Glow No, no, of course not. Very well. When?
Boxclever In a few minutes. Now, you'll have to wear a pinstripe suit and
  a false beard. Patients of Mrs Grimley-Cloned's generation all expect
  specialists to have beards.
Glow Specialist? I'm not a specialist. And this is the only suit I possess.
Boxclever (*ushering him out* UL) Well, we'll let the suit pass but you must
  have the beard or you'll have no credibility in her eyes.
Glow I'm not sure.

  Glow exits

Boxclever Of course you are.

*Bountiful registers distress, but pulls herself together as she enters the
surgery. She is dressed in the white suit*

  Mrs Grimley-Cloned enters the waiting-room

Ah, Nurse, would you see if Mrs Grimley-Cloned has arrived.
Bountiful Yes, Doctor. (*She goes into the waiting-room*)

The Lights come up on the waiting-room

Mrs Grimley-Cloned, Doctor will see you now.

*Mrs Grimley-Cloned follows Bountiful into the surgery. The Lights fade on
the waiting-room*

Boxclever Thank you, Nurse. I'll call you if I want you.

*Bountiful goes into the dispensary and sits filling in forms. Mrs Grimley-
Cloned sits*

(*Rising*) My dear Mrs Grimley-Cloned, how are you today?

Mrs Grimley-Cloned I try not to complain, Doctor.

Boxclever (*crossing to her* R) You are so brave, dear lady, so very brave. But I have some excellent news for you. Two pieces: the jollop, I mean, the elixir, has arrived and I have secured the services of one of our top consultants.

Mrs Grimley-Cloned You dear, dear boy. I shall remember you in my will.

Boxclever (*walking* DR *away from her*) Oh, come, come, dear Lady. There is no need to talk of wills.

Mrs Grimley-Cloned One never knows. If I should have a sudden relapse I might not be capable of altering it to my present wishes.

Boxclever (*returning to her* R, *quickly*) Yes, well, on the other hand, you are right of course. Perhaps you could drop in on your solicitor immediately you leave here.

Mrs Grimley-Cloned And so I shall. Cousin Herbert thinks he will have it all but he cares nothing for me. Do you know, he called me a hypochondriac.

Boxclever The thoughtless little beast, hitting the nail on the head like that.

Mrs Grimley-Cloned What?

Boxclever That's what I'd like to do to him. Hit his head on a bed of nails. It's a medieval torture.

Mrs Grimley-Cloned I can't bear violence of any sort. Even in such a good cause.

Boxclever Nor I, dear lady. I was speaking metaphorically, of course. (*He takes the bottle of jollop from his pocket*) But just see what I have here.

Mrs Grimley-Cloned (*ecstatically*) Oh, oh, is that the elixir?

Boxclever Smuggled from Japan.

Mrs Grimley-Cloned It looks a bit like the medicine I had as a child.

Boxclever Looks can be deceptive. That, dear lady, is the product of a thousand glands.

Mrs Grimley-Cloned Good Heavens. Could I have a dose now, do you think?

Boxclever I daren't open it until I have paid for it.

Mrs Grimley-Cloned I have a cheque for five thousand, made out to you.

Boxclever Ah, well, in that case——

She hands the cheque to him. He kisses it and places it in his top pocket

I'm sure it will be all right. (*He takes a plastic spoon from his pocket and is about to pour the jollop into it*)

Mrs Grimley-Cloned Not in a plastic spoon, Doctor. I am allergic to plastic.

Boxclever Oh dear, I'm afraid I——

Mrs Grimley-Cloned (*rummaging in her handbag again*) Never mind. I always carry a silver spoon or two, just in case.

Boxclever (*taking it*) Of course, how insensitive of me. (*He pours the jollop* *into the silver spoon and feeds it to her. He then rubs the spoon on his coat and pockets it)* Well?

Mrs Grimley-Cloned Um, it's very sweet.

Boxclever That's the goodness in it.

Mrs Grimley-Cloned Ah yes, I can feel it throbbing through my veins.

Boxclever Excellent.

There is a knock on the door and Dr Glow enters UL, now wearing an obviously false beard

Ah, Sir Lancelot, *(he moves to Glow's R)* I'm so pleased you could make it.

Mrs Grimley-Cloned *(rising and turning)* Sir Lancelot? Not Sir Lancelot Sprat?

Boxclever No, this is Sir Lancelot Prat, a distant cousin.

Glow *(pushing Boxclever across to DR)* Can we get on, Boxclever. My time is precious, you know.

Boxclever *(under his breath to Glow)* All right, no need to go OTT.

Mrs Grimley-Cloned *(moving to Glow's R, taking his hand)* Oh, Sir Lancelot, this is a pleasure indeed. I was worried in case you turned out to be some awful National Health doctor trying to make ends meet by giving second opinions. But I can see by your manner that you are used to dealing only with the best people.

Glow *(trying to extract his hand)* Quite right, Mrs Grimley-Cloned, I deal only with real people.

Mrs Grimley-Cloned How very gratifying to know that those hands of yours have never been in contact with the lower orders.

Glow *(wrenching his hand away)* Could we get this over with, Boxclever.

During the following, Glow makes to escape through the door DR

Boxclever *(ushering Mrs Grimley-Cloned to the couch)* Let me help you to the couch, dear lady, and…

He catches Glow and thrusts him behind the screens

…Sir Lancelot will give you a thorough examination. *(He helps her to the couch)*

Mrs Grimley-Cloned Ooh, careful, Doctor! Oh, Sir Lancelot, if only I could begin to tell you what I'm suffering.

Glow I'm sure you will, Mrs Grimley-Cloned, I'm sure you will.

Boxclever drops DR and paces back and forth while we hear Mrs Grimley-Cloned and Dr Glow from behind the screen

Mrs Grimley-Cloned I always feel more at ease with the nobility, don't you, Sir Lancelot? As I said to Lady Fleasedale, at the Hunt Ball—were you there, at Cleethorpe Hall, Sir Lancelot? I don't remember seeing you. Ooh, that was cold! We first met at a Royal Garden Party, you know. Lady Fleasedale and I, that is. I think you'll find my blood pressure quite terrible.

Glow Any pain here?

Mrs Grimley-Cloned Where?

Glow Here.

Mrs Grimley-Cloned Oh, simply agonizing. Of course the Duke and I are on Christian name terms. Yes, and I do mean the Duke.

Glow Any trouble with your joints?

Mrs Grimley-Cloned Do you know what he calls me? His little Triffid. Isn't that quaint?

Glow Your joints?

Mrs Grimley-Cloned What about them?

Glow Are they satisfactory?

Mrs Grimley-Cloned Of course they are. Cook sees to all that. She knows her meat all right. When you entertain in my circle only the best will do and she——

Glow No, your joints. Your knees, elbows, shoulders, ankles...

Mrs Grimley-Cloned Oh, I see. Silly me. I get so carried away. No, they're all seizing up. What am I to do, Sir Lancelot?

Glow Just lie back and rest for a moment while I consult with Dr Boxclever. (*He emerges from behind the screens and moves down to Boxclever*) Why am I wasting my time with this woman? There's nothing wrong with her that a plain diet and a bit of exercise wouldn't cure.

Boxclever (*jumping up and ushering him* DL *to just outside the dispensary door*) My dear chap, please keep your voice down.

Bountiful rises from the table in the dispensary and listens at the door

Glow You knew that, didn't you?

Boxclever She's suffering from over-indulgence. If we don't help to remove some of her surplus wealth, she'll only use it to harm her health further. We have a duty to protect her from herself.

Glow It is not ethical.

Boxclever Would you advocate more rich food, more alcohol, more jewellery to carry around? By leaving her with too much floating cash we are condemning her to a life of obesity. Worse, we are shortening her life by a decade.

Glow Well, put like that.

Bountiful reacts

Boxclever And if we can channel some of that surplus to where it is really needed.

The heavenly voices sound again and we hear Rosebud's voice on tape

Rosebud's Voice …into the streets unless we pay him a thousand pounds.
Glow So sometimes the end can justify the means?
Boxclever (*taking a cheque from his pocket and placing it in his hand*) Exactly, my dear chap. (*He takes his arm and propels him up to the door* UL *speaking loudly*) Thank you so much, Sir Lancelot, I look forward to receiving your report.

Glow exits

Mrs Grimley-Cloned (*emerging from behind the screen*) Oh, has Sir Lancelot gone?
Boxclever (*ushering her out* DR) Yes, dear lady, but I shall have his report within the week.
Mrs Grimley-Cloned Such a thorough man, I'm sure he will get to the bottom of my trouble.

Mrs Grimley-Cloned exits

Boxclever (*returning and calling*) Nurse, nurse!
Bountiful (*coming from the dispensary, dabbing her eyes with her handkerchief*) Yes, Doctor.
Boxclever Would you see if Mr Trusting is here.
Bountiful Yes, Doctor.

Bountiful makes her way to the waiting-room. As she does so, the Lights come up there

Ted enters in a wheelchair. He has a red blanket over his legs

Oh, Mr Trusting, you are here. Doctor will see you now.
Ted Thank you, Nurse.

She pushes him into the surgery. The Lights fade on the waiting-room

Boxclever (*moving to Ted and shaking his hand*) Mr Trusting, how are you today?
Ted Mustn't grumble, Doctor.
Boxclever (*to Bountiful*) Nurse, would you fetch the crutches from the dispensary?

Bountiful Yes, Dr Design.
Boxclever Pardon?
Bountiful For a moment I——
Boxclever Who is this Design?
Bountiful Only a character in a novel, *The Body Shop.*
Ted I've heard of that.
Boxclever Yes, but we must keep our minds on realities. Did you pay by
cheque, Mr Trusting? The crutches, Nurse, if you please!
Bountiful Yes, Doctor. (*She goes into the dispensary*)
Ted No, I paid cash. Mr Prune said he preferred it.
Boxclever Charged you VAT, I suppose?
Ted Oh yes.
Boxclever It was the amount I said?
Ted Except for the surcharges.
Boxclever Surcharges?
Ted For the headphones and taped music.
Boxclever Ah. Er, how much is he adding now? I need to know for future
quotes, you understand.
Ted Fifty pounds. Bit of a waste really as I was unconscious the whole time.
Boxclever (*taking out a small note book and writing*) Twenty per cent of
fifty—they treated you well in hospital, I trust?
Ted Oh, yes Doctor, I had every luxury.

Bountiful returns with the crutches

Boxclever Good, good. Well, you get what you pay for, don't you? (*He takes
the crutches from Bountiful*) Thank you, Nurse. I shan't require you
further.
Bountiful Very well, Doctor. I'll just finish off the forms for Dr Glow. (*She
goes into the dispensary*)
Boxclever Spend most of their time filling up forms as far as I can see. (*He
pushes the crutches at him*) Now, my dear chap, try these for size.

*Boxclever hands him the crutches and then removes his blanket which he
holds in front of Ted while he struggles to stand. He then imitates a Spanish
matador baiting the bull before he whips it away to reveal Ted standing on
one leg*

Ole! Yes, they appear to be fine. Very reasonably priced at five hundred
too. That bunion pain has gone completely, I trust?
Ted Yes, Doctor.
Boxclever You sure it was Prune? Looks more of a Hacker job to me.
Ted No, it was Prune. I remember seeing his name on the bill. Mind you I
was squinting with those bright operating theatre lights in my eyes.

Boxclever I just hope you could see to count out the cash.

Ted A nurse kindly did it for me.

Boxclever That's the big difference. Nothing's too much trouble when you go private. Prune's very good though. Gives a fair rake off. I mean—does a pretty fair take off.

Ted I find losing a leg very inconvenient, Doctor, especially when I'm so keen on sports. I only hope it was absolutely necessary.

Boxclever holds the blanket in front of Ted again so he can sit

Boxclever (*taking the crutches from him*) Of course it was necessary. There are some very nasty little bugs in the soil, you know, all ready to creep up your legs so you've doubled the odds of catching anything, haven't you? (*He places the crutches on the desk and returns to behind the chair*) Of course, to be really safe, it would pay you to have the other trimmed. You'd then have no direct contact with the soil and wouldn't that be an advantage?

Ted Well, in one way I suppose, but I can't help thinking——

Boxclever (*wheeling him in a circle* DS, *across* L *then* R *and up to the door* UL) Ah, but when it comes to medical matters, it's very dangerous for the layman to think. A little knowledge is a dangerous thing.

Ted Yes, but——

Boxclever And that's what you pay me for, isn't it?

Ted Well, yes, I suppose——

Boxclever Of course it is. Now don't you worry, I'll book you in to have that other troublesome leg off and in no time at all, you'll be A1 again. (*He wheels him up to the door* UL) With any luck I can get Prune or Hacker to complete the job today or tomorrow.

Ted Can I think it over, Doctor?

Boxclever Can't have the grass growing under your feet, can we? (*He laughs*) But then it won't be able to, will it?

Boxclever wheels Ted out UL. *As he does so, Rosebud enters through the waiting-room and looks anxiously around*

Bountiful stops filling in her forms and crosses to the door of the dispensary which she opens a little in order to see what is going on

Boxclever comes back

(*To Rosebud*) What are you doing here?

Rosebud (*dropping her sweet voice*) I want ter know when I gets me commission. I'm fed up doin' dirty work fer you. I ain't seen a penny yet.

Boxclever I've not found your work very satisfactory, that's why.

Rosebud Oh, an' who conned old Lady Fleasedale in ter seein' yer?

Boxclever Yes, but she hasn't come across with any of the readies yet.

Rosebud That ain't my fault, is it?

Boxclever And I'm a bit short. Just paid young Glow a thousand. Now if you could get it back off him for me, I can pay you.

Rosebud Right. Be like takin' sweets from a toddler. I'll get the cheque but I'll want cash, mind, an' none o' your funny business.

The Lights fade as Bountiful registers her shock at such villainy

CURTAIN

ACT II

SCENE 1

The same, two months later

When the CURTAIN *rises, the Lights come up on the waiting-room, where Mrs Spout, now imminently pregnant, is sitting*

Mrs Grimley-Cloned enters

Mrs Spout Here, you've got it wrong. It's only Dr Glow on today. None o' your toffee-nosed, private patients, thank you very much.

Mrs Grimley-Cloned I think I told you, my good woman, that I do not make mistakes.

Mrs Spout Don't you "my good woman" me! I ain't yer good woman!

Mrs Grimley-Cloned I mean what I say. Well, perhaps you're not a good woman. Perhaps——

Mrs Spout And what is you assassinating?

Mrs Grimley-Cloned What a delightful thought.

Mrs Spout Eh?

Mrs Grimley-Cloned It doesn't matter. No, actually, I'm here to see Dr Glow.

Mrs Spout Oh, how the high and mighty have fallen. So her ladyship has come down to goin' on the National Health, 'as she?

Mrs Grimley-Cloned Good heavens, no.

The Lights come up on the surgery

Dr Glow enters UL, *wearing a new pinstripe suit, and sits at his desk*

Nurse Bountiful, now wearing the split skirt etc. but with a plain cap, enters through the dispensary, looks at him, dabs her eye and goes to look in the waiting-room. She then returns to above Glow

Bountiful There's that Mrs Spout. Oh, and Mrs Grimley-Cloned has also arrived.

Glow Has she? She's more than half an hour early. Well, you better show her in.

Bountiful Hadn't you better see Mrs Spout? I mean——
Glow Mrs Grimley-Cloned, please, Nurse!
Bountiful Very well, Doctor. (*She crosses to the waiting-room*) Mrs
  Grimley-Cloned, Doctor will see you now.
Mrs Spout (*rising*) Here, who says?
Bountiful Dr Glow decides who he will see.
Mrs Spout Don't he know there's a queue.
Bountiful You must leave these decisions to Doctor.
Mrs Spout Well, I ain't see! I know what's right and I'm goin' ter see he does
  an' all. Get nothin' in this world if yer don't stand up fer yer rights. (*She
  pushes Bountiful aside and rushes into the surgery*)

| **Bountiful** | | But you can't! |
| **Mrs Grimley-Cloned** | (*together*) | How dare you! |

Dr Glow rises as Mrs Spout bursts in

Mrs Spout (*to Dr Glow*) What's this then, takin' private patients and makin'
  yer regulars wait?
Glow Mrs Spout, how dare you burst into my surgery like this!
Mrs Spout Oh, I dares, when I 'as to.

The following dialogue overlaps

Glow Kindly leave my surgery at once!
Bountiful (*rushing in and grabbing Mrs Spout's arm*) Will you do as Doctor
  says!
Mrs Grimley-Cloned (*collapsing on to the bench in the waiting-room*) Oh,
  my heart! My heart!

*Glow rushes to Mrs Spout's L, trying to assist Nurse Bountiful in ejecting the
irate Mrs Spout*

Glow At once, I say!
Bountiful You heard, Doctor!

They struggle with her

Mrs Spout I know me rights! (*She clutches her abdomen*) Oh, oh, ooh!

Dr Glow and Bountiful both stop, step back and stare at her

Bountiful Goodness, she's——
Glow She's about to——

Mrs Spout Now look what you've been an' gone an' done!
Glow Help her into my lounge, Nurse and ring the hospital!
Bountiful But, Doctor——
Glow Do as I say!
Bountiful (*to Mrs Spout*) Take my arm!

Bountiful helps Mrs Spout towards the door UL

Mrs Spout Don't worry, Doc. Probably a false alarm.
Bountiful (*without conviction*) Doctor will see you're all right.

Bountiful and Mrs Spout exit

Glow takes a clothes brush from his desk and brushes himself down. Then he crosses to the waiting-room

Glow (*seeing the recumbent Mrs Grimley-Cloned*) Oh, my dear Mrs Grimley-Cloned, whatever has happened?
Mrs Grimley-Cloned (*feigning coming to*) Where am I?
Glow Don't worry, dear lady, I am here.
Mrs Grimley-Cloned Oh, it's you, dear Dr Glow.
Glow I am here, dear lady.
Mrs Grimley-Cloned Oh, thank goodness. The noise, that dreadful woman, I——
Glow Let me help you through. We'll soon have you right as rain.

He helps her into the surgery and sits her in the chair in front of his desk. He then stands behind her and massages her neck. The Lights fade on the waiting-room

Mrs Grimley-Cloned Dear Dr Glow. You know, I think I even prefer you to Dr Boxclever, lovely man as he is.
Glow You are equally valuable to us both.
Mrs Grimley-Cloned As a case or as a person, Doctor?
Glow Both, dear lady. We are not merely concerned with your wealth—I mean, your health—but with——
Mrs Grimley-Cloned Little me as a——
Glow Purse. I mean, person. (*He moves down to her* R) But tell me, how has Dr Boxclever's pink jollop—elixir been? Has it helped?
Mrs Grimley-Cloned (*sighing*) I think I do feel a little better but I expect it will take time, Doctor, won't it?
Glow Boxclever will guarantee it. The elixir, I mean. I only wish, though, that he had consulted me because there is a more advanced treatment in Russia.

Mrs Grimley-Cloned Oh, is there? Dr Boxclever said this was the very latest.

Glow Yes, but he wouldn't have known. He's not in the forefront of research as I am.

Mrs Grimley-Cloned Oh, I was led to understand——

Glow But it is not for me——

Mrs Grimley-Cloned This Russian treatment, is it available?

Glow In ten years, possibly. Of course, I—no that would not be ethical.

Mrs Grimley-Cloned You could obtain it, couldn't you?

Glow Well, I have a little, sent me for experimental purposes but I dare not use it. I am accountable for every drop.

Mrs Grimley-Cloned Bribe someone. Everyone has their price; except English doctors of course.

Glow (*turning away from her*) I couldn't.

Mrs Grimley-Cloned Offer them ten thousand.

Glow (*turning back*) I could.

Nurse Bountiful rushes in from UL

Bountiful Quick, Doctor, Mrs Spout is about to give birth on your settee!

Glow (*ignoring her, still speaking to Mrs Grimley-Cloned*) Ten thousand. It is yours, dear lady. (*He moves towards the dispensary*) I'll get it at once.

Bountiful (*following him into the dispensary*) You must come! If you don't I can't answer for the consequences!

Glow continues to ignore Bountiful and takes a gallon jar of green jollop and a small medicine bottle out of the cupboard and carefully fills the bottle from the jar

Please, Dr Glow, Herman, leave this until later. We have an emergency on our hands!

Pause

Oh, what has become of you? You used to be so kind, so considerate. Your patients always came first. You were Dr Glory in *The Saviour of the Slums* but now you only think of how much money you can make. You've even sunk to swindling; selling worthless jollop.

Pause

I know what started it. It was that charlatan, Boxclever, and his accomplice, Rosebud.

The mention of Rosebud elicits the first response from Glow

Oh yes, you didn't know that, did you? She's not the sweet, little thing you
thought. She's in with Boxclever. I've seen them plotting.

Glow Stop! How dare you sully the name of dearest Rosebud! You are an
insanely jealous woman, Nurse Bountiful, who cannot separate fact from
fiction and I regret to say, no longer fit to serve in my clinic. Take a month's
salary and go!

Bountiful No, I will stay and somehow save you from your own stupidity.
You cannot fire me. I am not your employee. But please, let this wait; the
baby won't!

Glow That woman doesn't need a doctor. She's young, well, comparatively
so, healthy and poor. You see to her, Nurse. I have more important things
to do.

Bountiful Very well, I will. I just hope that it's a straightforward birth or you
will have much to answer for.

Bountiful runs out of the dispensary to the door UL, *but collides with*
Boxclever as he enters

Glow continues to pour out his green jollop

Boxclever Steady, Nurse, steady! Have you seen Glow?
Bountiful Excuse me, Doctor, I must——
Boxclever Just drop in to make a few arrangements and end up delivering
some wretched woman in Glow's lounge.
Bountiful You delivered her?
Boxclever Yes and I bet I won't see a penny piece for it either.
Bountiful Oh, ooh!

Bountiful runs off UL

Boxclever (*becoming aware of Mrs Grimley-Cloned, crossing to her* R) Mrs
Grimley-Cloned, dear lady, what are you doing here today? Our appointment
is for tomorrow.
Mrs Grimley-Cloned Oh, dear Dr Boxclever. I have only popped in for
some more of your wonderful elixir. I thought nice Dr Glow would oblige
me.
Boxclever Dr Glow! What does that mountebank know of my pink jollop,
I mean, the elixir?
Mrs Grimley-Cloned He said he couldn't supply it.
Boxclever I should hope so. Some ethics survive at least.
Mrs Grimley-Cloned But he knew of something even better.
Boxclever What?

Glow enters from the dispensary, carrying the small bottle of green jollop

Glow Here we are, my dear Mrs Grimley-Cloned. (*He sees Boxclever*) Oh, I didn't expect——
Boxclever Obviously, Glow. How dare you prescribe for my patient?
Glow (*rushing to Mrs Grimley-Cloned's* L) Your patient?
Mrs Grimley-Cloned Boys, boys, please! Don't quarrel over me. I need you both.
Boxclever Yes, my patient!
Glow I thought we were partners now?
Boxclever That does not include sharing my most lucrative patient.
Mrs Grimley-Cloned Lucrative? What does he mean by that?
Glow Lucid. He means lucid, able to tell him of symptoms, in a most lucid manner.
Mrs Grimley-Cloned Then why did he say, "lucrative"?
Glow He has trouble with words, slightly dyslexic, you know.
Mrs Grimley-Cloned Oh, I didn't know. Poor Dr Boxclever. It's not catching, is it?
Glow No, no, just a little impairment. Nothing serious.
Boxclever I'm still waiting for an explanation, Glow.
Glow (*moving into the dispensary*) Come into the dispensary, Dr Boxclever. We can better discuss Mrs Grimley-Cloned's case there.
Mrs Grimley-Cloned Oh dear, does that mean it's too awful for me to hear about?
Boxclever No, no, dear lady, just highly technical, that's all. Don't want to worry you. Easy to get the wrong end of the stick if you're not a medico. (*He goes into the dispensary*) Right, Glow, this had better be good.

Nurse Bountiful enters UL, *just in time to see them disappear into the dispensary*

She is about to follow them in when she is stopped by hearing Glow's next speech. She waits at the door, listening. The Lights cross-fade to the dispensary

Glow The game's up, Boxclever.
Boxclever What?
Glow You've been found out. I've been investigating your background and I have discovered that not only are you not on the Medical Register but that your name is not Boxclever. It's Monty Bank, who as far as I can ascertain—has no qualifications in anything.
Boxclever You've got the wrong man, I'm afraid, my dear Glow.
Glow It's no good trying to bluff it out, Bank, I have documentary evidence.
Boxclever Then you might as well know that Bank is just one of my aliases.

My real name is Wiley and I was a doctor once but got struck off through no fault of my own.

Glow Really?

Boxclever I was discovered in bed with a young female patient.

Glow Ah.

Boxclever She was suffering from hypothermia. There was no other way of warming her.

Glow An unusual complaint for a young female, wouldn't you say?

Boxclever You are as sceptical as the BMA. Don't you think I should have been given the benefit of the doubt?

Glow They evidently had no doubts.

Boxclever It's easy for you. You don't know what it's like to be deprived of your vocation, of your livelihood. Look, we can come to an understanding. I'll see you get a bigger cut.

Glow Don't try to bribe me, Wiley, Bank, Boxclever, whatever your name is. It won't wash. I'm incorruptible.

There is a big sigh of relief from Nurse Bountiful

From now on, I'm the one who calls the shots. You are working for me now and I'll expect fifty percent of all you make.

Boxclever Fifty?

Glow Take it or leave it.

A reaction of despair from Bountiful as she runs off UL

Boxclever You win, Glow, curse you! For the time being that is.

Glow Good, glad to see you're being so sensible about it. Now, come in with me and help me make a killing with the green jollop. It's the latest thing from Russia, you understand. (*He leads the way back into the surgery and crosses to Mrs Grimley-Cloned's* L)

Boxclever follows, going to her R. *The Lights cross-fade to the surgery*

My dear Mrs Grimley-Cloned, so sorry to keep you waiting but such a complex case as yours deserves our fullest discussion.

Mrs Grimley-Cloned Dear boys.

Glow Dr Boxclever and I are of one opinion. Eh, Boxclever?

Boxclever Yes, yes, Dr Glow has persuaded me that the Russian treatment is better. Frightfully expensive, of course, but infinitely superior.

Mrs Grimley-Cloned How can I thank you both for such dedication?

Glow Your complete recovery will be thanks enough.

Boxclever In about fifteen year's time.

Glow Or twenty. (*He produces the small bottle of green jollop*) Here it is. Every drop they've been able to send me.

Boxclever Good heavens, so much! It must be worth a fortune.

Glow I contracted to pay ten thousand should I use it all.

Mrs Grimley-Cloned You shall have my cheque immediately.

Glow No hurry, dear lady, but immediately would be the most convenient. Eh, Boxclever?

Boxclever We poor physicians cannot put such amounts up front, I'm afraid.

Mrs Grimley-Cloned (*opening her handbag*) No, of course not. I shall write you a cheque this instant. I couldn't have my dear boys in debt on my account, could I?

Boxclever Not likely.

Mrs Grimley-Cloned Pardon?

Glow He means it would be so unlike a lady of quality.

Mrs Grimley-Cloned (*smiling*) But of course.

They hover over her as she starts to write the cheque

Ted enters through the waiting-room in his wheelchair. He has now, apparently, had the other leg removed

Ted Boxclever, you dirty, money-grubbing swine!

Boxclever (*opening the door*) Ah, Mr Trusting! Now——

Ted Don't try to flannel me. I now know what you are: you're a——

Boxclever (*shouting above him and grabbing the chair*) Keep calm, Mr Trusting, keep calm! (*He wheels him into the dispensary*) It will soon pass——

Ted		You won't get away with it!
Boxclever	(*together*)	Soon find you a little sedative.
Mrs Grimley-Cloned		Good gracious!
Glow		Who the hell…?

Boxclever pops his head back from the dispensary with one hand clamped firmly over Ted's mouth

Boxclever A psychiatric case, soon have him sedated.

During the next few lines of dialogue, Boxclever binds and gags Ted with bandages taken from the dispensary cupboard

Mrs Grimley-Cloned Good heavens, I didn't know Dr Boxclever dealt with people of that sort.

Glow (*crossing L, trying to peer into the dispensary*) He is such a compassionate man.

Mrs Grimley-Cloned Compassion is an admirable quality, but it should be kept within one's class, otherwise it becomes indulgence. Don't you agree, Dr Glow?

Glow (*moving back to her* R) Oh, certainly agree with one rule for the rich.

Mrs Grimley-Cloned Not that I am unfeeling about the poor, but if we do too much for them, they will never stand on their own two feet. (*She points at the dispensary*) That man's a case in point.

Glow We'll never get him to stand on his own two feet now, I fear.

Mrs Grimley-Cloned Quite. Now, where was I?

Glow Uhm, you were writing the cheque.

Mrs Grimley-Cloned So I was. Now who should I make it out to?

Boxclever emerges from the dispensary

Glow It would be easier made out to——

Boxclever (*rushing forward to Mrs Grimley-Cloned's* L) Both of us!

Mrs Grimley-Cloned Boxclever and Glow?

Glow No, Glow and Boxclever.

Boxclever He's the senior partner.

Mrs Grimley-Cloned (*writing*) I didn't know you worked together. It's so convenient to have my two boys in the one place.

Rosebud, holding a glass necklace in her hand, bursts in from the waiting-room

She bears down on Boxclever who retreats across L as she advances upon him

Rosebud Bloody paste! That's what it is, bloody paste! You slimy little toad Boxclever, thought you could pay me off with a few glass beads, did you? Well, nobody gets over Liza Kimbo, I can tell you.

Glow Liza Kimbo? I thought you were Rosebud?

Rosebud Yes, Ducky, well we can all have our fantasies, can't we?

Boxclever A rosebud by any other name——

Rosebud Don't you get clever with me. I've got the drop on you all right. (*To Mrs Grimley-Cloned*) He ain't no bloody doctor. He's a conman. Have the skin off your back while he's smilin' at yer.

Mrs Grimley-Cloned Oh, oh, my heart, my heart! (*She faints, dropping the cheque as she does so*)

Glow Help me get her on the couch, Boxclever.

They lift her on to the couch. Rosebud picks up the cheque as they do so

Boxclever We must convince her she's had a dream.

Rosebud She's not had a dream; she's had a bloody nightmare. (*She looks at the cheque and moves up to them*) What's this then? Ten grand, made out to both of yer. You disappoint me, Dr Glow. Thought you was straight. Taken me last illusion, you have.

Glow And you mine. Is there no innocence left?

Rosebud (*pointing at the recumbent Mrs Grimley-Cloned*) Only her and that stupid nurse of yours.

Boxclever (*advancing on her*) Give me the cheque, Rosebud—er—Liza.

Rosebud (*retreating before him and backing round the desk*) Rosebud will do. I rather like it. For a while I almost believed... Goin' soft in the head, I am. (*She holds the cheque behind her back and backs away from him*)

Boxclever Come along now. It's no good to you.

Rosebud I could tear it up.

Boxclever No, you wouldn't.

Rosebud Pay you out for your bloody necklace.

Boxclever It was a mistake. I gave you the wrong one.

Rosebud Too true you did.

Glow snatches the cheque from behind her

Boxclever Well done, Glow! You're learning fast.

Rosebud Right! Now you're both goin' ter get it! I'll blow the gaff on both of yer.

Boxclever Now, now, Liza, two can play at that game. What about the Fleasedale jewels then?

Rosebud How did you know about that?

Boxclever I've got a whole file on you, my girl. It's a hobby of mine, collecting facts about my friends. Comes in very useful at times.

Rosebud Bastard! (*She moves to exit* DR) You haven't heard the last of me. Just wait and see.

Rosebud exits

Boxclever That was lucky.

Glow Lucky?

Boxclever Intuitive guess on my part. Now, I think we'd better get this cheque paid in, just in case the dream idea fails. You give the old girl a sedative while I pop this (*he takes the cheque*) down to the bank.

Glow (*snatching it back*) No, you give her the sedative, I'll take the cheque.

Boxclever (*snatching it back again*) You're the qualified doctor. I don't wish to contravene the law. I won't be a tick.

Boxclever runs off

Dr Glow dashes after him, stops at the door, dashes back and pulls the screens around Mrs Grimley-Cloned and then follows him out

Nurse Bountiful enters UL, *looks around and then goes down to the dispensary door and knocks*

Ted is galvanised into making incoherent noises through his gag

Bountiful Is that you, Dr Glow?

More incoherent noises from Ted

It doesn't sound like you. (*She tries the door and then seeing the key is in the lock, opens it to find Ted. She dashes in and wheels him out into the surgery*) Oh, you poor man. It's Mr Trusting, isn't it?

Ted tries to answer but only makes a moaning noise through the bandage around his face. Bountiful takes it off

(*Taking off the bandage*) What has that dreadful Dr Boxclever had done to you? I'm sure there was nothing wrong with your legs.
Ted (*throwing off the blanket and shooting out his legs*) No, Nurse Bountiful, there is nothing wrong with my legs. (*He gets out of the chair and takes her hand*) Ted Rooter, investigative journalist.

Black-out

SCENE 2

The same. The action is continuous

Bountiful Oh, Mr Rooter, you're the answer to my prayers. You're like Clint Halo in *The Best In The West*. Have you read it?
Ted I'm a journalist. Do you expect me to read other people's scribblings?
Bountiful Dr Boxclever isn't a doctor. He was struck off.
Ted I know.
Bountiful And now he's corrupted dear Dr Glow. You must save him.
Ted That depends on whether Glow co-operates.
Bountiful He will, he will; I know he will. But Boxclever has a hold over him. He's like the Master in *Fanfare for Megalomania*. You must get poor Dr Glow out of his clutches. Promise you will.
Ted I'll do what I can but if he's mixed up in this Dupo racket that is bringing

the whole of private medicine into disrepute, he'll have to take the rap along with Boxclever.

There is a snort from Mrs Grimley-Cloned from behind the screens

What the…? (*He draws back the screens to reveal Mrs Grimley-Cloned*)
Mrs Grimley-Cloned (*sitting bolt upright*) Stop! Stop!
Bountiful (*rushing to her and supporting her*) There, there, I'm here.
Mrs Grimley-Cloned (*clinging to her*) Oh, Nurse, Nurse, I've had such a nightmare. I dreamed that dear Dr Boxclever was, was——
Ted (*moving in to her*) A crook.
Mrs Grimley-Cloned Well, yes. But how…? (*She recognizes Ted*) Oh, it's you. How can I take your word for anything? You're a nut, aren't you? Oh, your legs!
Ted Yes, I'm not nutty enough to let your precious Dr Boxclever talk me out of those and I don't pay thousands for pink and green jollop.
Mrs Grimley-Cloned Are you referring to my elixir, my good man?
Ted (*crossing to the dispensary*) Elixir, my foot. I'll show you your precious elixir, in great quantities.
Mrs Grimley-Cloned He is raving. Tell me it's not true, Nurse.
Bountiful If only I could.

Ted returns carrying the two gallon jars of pink and green jollop, which he deposits on the desk

Ted Here's your elixir. There's probably a five gallon drum out the back somewhere.
Mrs Grimley-Cloned (*sliding off the couch and coming down to sit in the chair*) Oh, oh, I've been duped. How shall I ever hold my head up again. (*She drops her head in her hands*) The Duchess will cut me dead.
Ted No, she'll love you for it.
Mrs Grimley-Cloned You mean?
Ted Yes, she's Boxclever's patient too.
Mrs Grimley-Cloned (*sitting up briskly*) Oh, I feel so much better.
Ted (*wheeling the wheelchair across to* RC) Right, there's no time to lose. We must get Boxclever and Glow to incriminate themselves.
Bountiful Not Dr Glow!
Ted We shall see. Now I intend to record every word they say.
Bountiful They may not come back.
Ted They'll be back to see if their golden goose can still be duped.
Mrs Grimley-Cloned (*standing*) Are you referring to me as a goose? (*She sits*) Dear me but perhaps I am a goose. I have been foolish, I admit. Mind you, I never really trusted that Boxclever. There's something about his eyes.

Marlene enters through the waiting-room

Ted We may not have long——
Marlene What's been happening here? I've just seen Glow chasing Boxclever down the street.
Bountiful You can't just walk in——
Ted It's all right, Nurse. This is Inspector Delve of Scotland Yard, the Fraud Squad.
Bountiful Oh, then that heart attack was——
Marlene Faked. Yes, all part of our training. But Dr Glow acted correctly. It should stand him in good stead at his trial.
Bountiful Trial? Oh.
Ted We don't know if Glow is implicated yet. That's why we need the recording. (*He takes two microphones from under the cushion on the wheelchair*) Now, these are radio mikes. (*He hands one to Marlene*) You'd better have one, Inspector and— (*to Mrs Grimley-Cloned*) Mrs Grimley-Cloned, the other. They're only effective within three to four feet so you'll need to secrete them about your person.
Marlene I have a special pocket.
Mrs Grimley-Cloned I'm afraid——
Ted (*thrusting the mike down her ample bosom*) That'll do the trick.
Mrs Grimley-Cloned Ooh, it tickles.
Ted Right, now Inspector, you go and sit in the waiting-room and if they come back, ask for a consultation. Say you're willing to pay. (*He sits in the wheelchair and tucks his legs under him*) I've had a recorder built into this chair. So, Nurse, if you'll tie me up again and wheel me into the dispensary——
Bountiful (*tying Ted up*) Dr Glow knew nothing about your operations. He would never have recommended amputation, you know. Dr Boxclever has hypnotised him. Has him under his influence, like Spenghastly in *Watch My Ding Dong*.
Ted I've not read that.
Bountiful Hypnotised his assistant with his swinging watch.
Ted I'm glad it was his watch.
Bountiful (*wheeling Ted back to the dispensary*) We must break Boxclever's spell.
Mrs Grimley-Cloned I'd like to break his head.
Ted Everyone to their places now.

Bountiful wheels Ted into the dispensary. Marlene goes and sits in the waiting-room. Mrs Grimley-Cloned vaults back on to the couch and draws the curtains

Bountiful I can't bear to stay and watch. I must go and see how poor Mrs Spout is getting on.

Ted tries to say something to her, but his gag reduces it to incoherent splutter

Don't worry, I'll be back.

Bountiful dashes off UL *then returns immediately, grabs the two bottles of jollop and returns them to the dispensary*

This is what you meant, wasn't it?

Ted nods

They won't come back. I know they won't.

Bountiful leaves Ted and runs off UL *sobbing*

Boxclever and Glow enter DR

Glow (*seeing Marlene*) You again. Sorry, can't see you. No more freebies. I've gone private.

Marlene But I want to be private. I don't mind paying for the best.

Boxclever You're Mrs Trusting?

Marlene That's right, Doctor. You treated my husband, Ted. Made a wonderful job of him, I must say.

Boxclever Ah yes. Legless Ted. Not won the Pools again, has he?

Marlene No, but we've still got a bit left.

Glow How big a bit?

Marlene Just a few thousand.

Boxclever I'm sure we can fit you in. What do you say, Glow?

Glow Of course we can. When did I ever turn a patient away. Just give us a few minutes to get rid of the old trout—I mean—a few minutes to settle our waiting patient.

Boxclever (*under his breath*) Settle her account.

Marlene What was that, Doctor? I'm afraid I'm a little hard of hearing.

Glow (*quickly*) Count her blood. He means: make a blood count.

Marlene I see.

Boxclever (*shouting at her*) We do a good line in hearing aids. Give you a third off.

Glow Let's cut out the commercials, Boxclever, and see how the old girl is.

Marlene I think you have a lovely voice, Dr Boxclever, just right for broadcasting.

Boxclever Thank you, my dear, but I'm afraid I'm absolutely scared stiff of microphones.

Marlene Well, that really is a pity.

Glow Boxclever!

Boxclever All right! Sorry, my dear, but we must get on. Won't keep you waiting long. (*He goes through into the dispensary and draws back the couch screens*)

Glow follows

(*Looking at the recumbent Mrs Grimley-Cloned*) Thank God, she's still out for the count.

Mrs Grimley-Cloned pretends to stir and then sits bolt upright

Mrs Grimley-Cloned Stop! Stop!

Boxclever (*taking her arm*) There, there, dear lady.

Mrs Grimley-Cloned (*turning to Boxclever*) Oh, it's you, Doctor. I think I must have just had a nightmare.

Boxclever Not uncommon, dear lady. It's the elixir, you see. It's very strong.

Mrs Grimley-Cloned (*sobbing*) It was terrible, terrible!

Boxclever Yes, yes.

Mrs Grimley-Cloned I dreamt that you and dear Dr Glow were just after my money.

Glow Heaven forbid.

Mrs Grimley-Cloned (*sliding off the couch and gripping both their arms*) I know, I know, it's unforgivable but I couldn't help it.

Glow and Boxclever help her to walk to DRC

Boxclever Hallucinations of this sort are not uncommon. Take that awful Rosebud person.

Mrs Grimley-Cloned I feel so badly about it. Especially when you both went to so much trouble to obtain the elixir for me.

Boxclever Think no more about it.

Mrs Grimley-Cloned To think that I should think that my two dear boys could... (*She thrusts her bosom at Boxclever*) Tell me you obtained the pink elixir from Japan and that it is a miracle drug.

Boxclever (*reeling back with surprise*) Of course I did and it is. At least I thought so until Dr Glow told me of the Russian discovery.

Nurse Bountiful enters UL

Mrs Grimley-Cloned (*thrusting her bosom at Glow*) Ah yes, of course. You supplied the green elixir, didn't you, Dr Glow?

Bountiful forces herself between Mrs Grimley-Cloned and Glow

Bountiful Dr Glow, you'll be pleased to know that mother and child are both doing well.

Glow Mother and child? What are you talking about, Nurse?

Bountiful Mrs Spout, of course.

Glow Oh, her.

Bountiful Aren't you concerned? She was your patient.

Glow Oh, yes, of course I'm concerned about all my patients.

Bountiful (*jumping out of the way and pushing Glow at Mrs Grimley-Cloned*) Oh, say that again, Doctor!

Glow What?

Bountiful That you're concerned.

Glow I'm concerned about all my patients.

A sigh of relief from Bountiful

The private ones, that is.

Bountiful cries out in despair and throws herself over the couch, sobbing

Mrs Grimley-Cloned (*drawing his head down on to her bosom*) Of course you are. And you did get the green elixir for me from Russia?

Glow Yes, yes and I'll get you more if you need it.

Boxclever Of course she'll need it. It's a long, slow treatment, Dr Glow.

Glow So it is, Dr Boxclever, so it is.

Mrs Grimley-Cloned I knew I could rely on my two boys to do the decent thing. (*She pats her bosom*) I think you've both done splendidly.

There is a loud burst of sobbing from Bountiful

Glow (*moving to the couch and drawing the curtains*) Do shut up, woman! (*He crosses to the desk*) Now, dear lady, shall we make you another appointment?

Boxclever (*darting across to below Glow*) Perhaps you feel in need of another second opinion?

Mrs Grimley-Cloned (*crossing to them, leaning across the desk*) Oh dear no, I trust my two boys implicitly. Though that specialist was very nice. Do you know, Dr Glow, without his beard, he would have been almost your double.

Boxclever Almost but not quite. Nature can be very perverse.

During the next few lines of dialogue, Marlene creeps in from the waiting-room and conceals herself behind the couch screen

Glow (*looking through the desk diary*) Shall we say in two weeks' time?

Boxclever Not so long, surely? There might be complications.
Mrs Grimley-Cloned Oh dear, isn't the elixir working?
Glow Not as fast as we'd like. Perhaps an operation——
Boxclever Cut out the dead wood.
Mrs Grimley-Cloned I beg your pardon?
Glow The infected parts. He was speaking metaphorically.

Mrs Grimley-Cloned pretends to be alarmed and sinks back on to the chair in front of the desk. Glow assists her and ends up on her R

Mrs Grimley-Cloned Oh dear.
Boxclever (*moving in to her* L) Only the tiniest of scars. Prune is very skilful.
Mrs Grimley-Cloned What parts? Don't I need all my bits?
Boxclever Sometimes better without.

During the next few lines of dialogue, Mrs Grimley-Cloned thrusts her bosom at whoever is talking

Mrs Grimley-Cloned This Mr Prune, does he work for Dupo?
Glow Or there's Hacker.
Boxclever Hacker for the big jobs; Prune for small bits.
Mrs Grimley-Cloned In your view, it's essential?
Boxclever Absolutely.
Mrs Grimley-Cloned Dr Glow?
Glow Unquestionably.

There is a loud burst of sobbing from Bountiful

What is wrong with that woman?
Boxclever She reads too many cheap novels. Well, think it over, dear lady, but don't hesitate too long: there's a special offer this month.
Mrs Grimley-Cloned Special offer?
Boxclever Cut price offer.
Mrs Grimley-Cloned You cannot put a price on health. Cost should be the last consideration.
Boxclever (*rubbing his hands together*) Absolutely. The sky's the limit, eh, Glow?
Glow Especially when it's cut three ways.
Mrs Grimley-Cloned Three ways?
Boxclever I told you Prune was incredibly skilful. He does the tiny, the minute and the totally invisible scar.
Glow You'd hardly know he'd touched you.
Boxclever You won't know you've had an operation.
Glow Until you get the bill.

Mrs Grimley-Cloned I must have time to think it over. It's so much harder for a woman. Scars can be so embarrassing and you never know what demands will be made by the next fashion: which bits we shall be required to expose.

Boxclever (*escorting her to the door*) Yes, yes, think it over, dear lady. Whatever you decide is fine by us. We are only here to lighten your load.

Glow sits at the desk as Boxclever leads Mrs Grimley-Cloned out through the waiting-room and then returns

(*Crossing* L *to the filing cabinet*) That wretched Mrs Trusting has gone. Wouldn't wait I suppose. Should have thought she was used to that on the NHS. Pity, could have been worth a bob or two.

Glow Her heart was in a poor state. I doubt if she could stand an operation.

Boxclever It's not payment by results, you know, and the insurance guarantees you get paid.

Glow She said she had money.

Boxclever (*going to the dispensary*) Her husband is going to need every penny of that. (*To Ted as he wheels him out and across to* RC) Aren't you, old sport?

Ted makes incoherent noises through his gag

Of course you are. There's nothing more I can do for you, you know. I really think you'd be better in a nursing home. Now, Dupo runs a very good one, The Last Post Nursing Home. Can I book you in? The food is excellent and there's a colour telly in every room.

More incoherent noises from Ted. Boxclever takes off his gag

I can't tell a word you're saying.

Ted (*throwing off his bonds and gag and spinning the chair around to face Boxclever*) The game's up, Boxclever!

Boxclever (*stepping back*) What?

Ted I'm not the fool you take me for. My name's not Trusting.

Boxclever You're not her husband?

Ted No.

Boxclever How very immoral. You did win the Pools though?

Ted No.

Boxclever No?

Ted No, I'm Ted Rooter, investigative journalist.

Boxclever You sneaky little... Trust the gutter press; go to any lengths. But you wouldn't...?

Ted (*shooting out his legs*) Not likely.

Boxclever (*backing up stage behind the desk*) How could you sink so low? There's no integrity left.

Ted (*moving to* URC) Prune and Hacker are already under arrest and Dupo has been closed down. So you might as well come clean.

Boxclever I don't know what you're talking about.

Ted It's no good, Boxclever, alias Bank or Wiley. The game is well and truly up. I have indisputable evidence.

Boxclever (*moving to above the desk*) It's your word against mine. No, better than that, it's your word against mine, Glow's and Nurse Bountiful's.

Ted Nurse Bountiful is on our side.

Boxclever Well, it's two doctors against one journalist and one nurse. Everyone knows what liars journalists are and as for Bountiful—she lives in a world of fantasy.

Glow (*rising and moving to* DR) No, Boxclever, you're on your own.

Boxclever What, turning Queen's evidence, are we, Glow? (*To Ted*) He put me up to it. He's Mr Master Mind. I'm only the puppet; it's Glow that pulls the strings.

Marlene whips back the curtains of the screen and emerges with the microphone in her hand. Nurse Bountiful sits on the couch wiping away tears of joy

Marlene That's too bad then because Dr Glow has been helping me and Special Branch to break this health racket and restore people's confidence in private medicine.

Boxclever What?

Glow Did you really think you could corrupt me, Boxclever?

Boxclever You were pretty convincing. What about neglecting Mrs Spout in her hour of need?

Glow That was the hardest moment but I couldn't reveal myself or my cover would have been blown.

Boxclever I'll deny everything.

Marlene You have condemned yourself. I've recorded every word.

Boxclever You?

Ted Yes, you've met the Inspector, haven't you?

Boxclever Inspector?

Ted Inspector Delve, of the Yard.

Boxclever (*darting for the door* DR) You'll never take me! I know how to disappear.

Boxclever dashes off DR

Ted Let him go; he won't get far.

Bountiful (*moving to above the desk*) Oh, how could I ever have doubted you?

Glow (*moving up to face her*) And how could I have been so blind? You're worth a thousand Rosebuds.

Bountiful I love you.

Glow And now I come to think about it, I love you too.

Mrs Grimley-Cloned enters DR, *frogmarching Boxclever before her*

Mrs Grimley-Cloned (*taking the microphone out of her bosom*) I went off with this. (*She shakes Boxclever*) And I caught this coming out of the door. I expect you'd like both back.

Glow Mrs Grimley-Cloned, I must apologise——

Mrs Grimley-Cloned Don't you apologise to me, you ghastly fraudulent doctor you. (*She shakes Boxclever*) You're quite as bad as he is.

Ted No, Mrs Grimley-Cloned, Dr Glow was only acting a part to catch Boxclever. He is a genuine doctor.

Mrs Grimley-Cloned Well, I'm glad someone is genuine at last.

Bountiful My Herman is. He's just like Mr Warmheart in *The Corrupt and the Corrupted*.

Mrs Spout enters UL *in a dressing gown and carrying her baby*

Mrs Spout Here, am I supposed to see ter meself then? Bloomin' National Health DIY, that's what it is.

Bountiful (*moving to her*) Oh, Mrs Spout, you shouldn't be out of bed!

Glow (*following*) No indeed. Let's get you back at once.

Bountiful and Dr Glow usher Mrs Spout to the exit

Mrs Spout So you're takin' an interest now, are you? And about bloomin' time too!

Bountiful, Dr Glow and Mrs Spout exit

Mrs Grimley-Cloned (*shaking Boxclever*) Just what shall I do with this?

Ted Give me a hand, Inspector. We'll tie him in the wheelchair. See how he likes being made immobile.

They tie Boxclever into the wheelchair

Mrs Grimley-Cloned (*flexing her forearms*) You know, I think I shall give up doctors. I didn't realize how strong I was until now. I might even go in for weight training. I rather fancy pumping iron, if that's the right expression. Quite the in thing, I believe.

Ted Well, you can start getting into condition by wheeling him down to the cop shop. (*To Marlene*) How about a quiet drink, Inspector, to compare notes?

Marlene I'm on duty but you can stand me a coffee. (*To Mrs Grimley-Cloned*) I'll give them a buzz to let them know you're bringing him in.

Marlene and Ted exit DR

Mrs Grimley-Cloned follows, wheeling Boxclever

Boxclever Dear lady, can't we come to some understanding?

Mrs Grimley-Cloned I understand you perfectly, Boxclever. Your eyes give you away.

Mrs Grimley-Cloned and Boxclever exit DR

The stage is empty for a second and then Widdell enters DR, *carrying a large bundle of forms*

He staggers across with them and dumps them on the desk. He sits in the doctor's chair, wiping his brow

Glow enters UL

Glow (*calling over his shoulder*) Just get my stethoscope, Mrs Spout. Won't be a second. (*He sees Widdell*) Oh.

Widdell It isn't good enough, you know, Glow, not at all.

Glow (*crossing to above the desk*) What isn't, Mr Widdell?

Widdell Productivity.

Glow Oh.

Widdell No, I have had to alter the schedules. You will now have three twenty-four hour shifts, consecutively, followed by half a day off.

Bountiful enters UL

Bountiful Excuse me, Doctor, but Reception want to know if you can fit another nine patients into your round. Oh, and Mrs Spout says you haven't kissed the baby.

The phone rings

Glow (*to Widdell, picking up the phone*) Excuse me.... (*Into the phone*) Yes, this is Dr Glow speaking——

As Glow speaks into the phone, the following speeches are said over

...I see and when did this happen? ... Well, put her to bed, give her aspirin and bathe her brow with tepid water. I'll call in just as soon as I can. ... No, no, I'm sure there's no cause for alarm. ... Yes, yes, I will, better to make quite sure.

Widdell Your prescriptions are still too high. Must I remind you that we no longer allow branded names. Not when there's a cheaper alternative. Costs have got to be kept in check. If you want more, you'll have to raise the money yourself. Have you thought about starting a "Friends of the Clinic"?

Mrs Spout (*off*) Doctor! Doctor!

Bountiful Can I have an answer, Doctor? Just nod your head.

Glow nods vigorously, Widdell rabbits on and Mrs Spout continues to call out as——

——the CURTAIN *falls*

FURNITURE AND PROPERTY LIST

Further dressing may be added at the director's discretion

ACT I

SCENE 1

On stage: WAITING-ROOM:
3 chairs
Pamphlets on "Looking after your heart"

DISPENSARY:
Table
Cupboard
Shelving

SURGERY:
Examination couch
Removable tatty screen
Plastic-topped desk. *On it*: phone, diary
2 cheap plastic chairs
Filing cabinet containing files in drawer
2 medical charts

Off stage: Briefcase, containing stethoscope, diary, menu, very large sports bag containing 2 gold-framed pictures, feather duster, smart white costume with split skirt and chic little nurse's cap with "Dupo" embroidered, vase of flowers, brochures, documents (**Boxclever**)
Small set of steps (**Workman 1**)
Pair of curtains on curtain pole (**Workman 2** and **Workman 3**)
Antique carver chair (**Workman 1**)
Antique desk (**Workman 2** and **Workman 3**)
New folding screen (**Workman 1**)
Handbag containing pen and cheque book (**Mrs Grimley-Cloned**)
Large briefcase containing notebook, huge bundle of forms (**Widdell**)

Personal: **Boxclever:** envelope
                Glow: stethoscope
                Widdell: identity card

SCENE 2

Set: Gallon jar of pink jollop
                Small medicine bottle

Off stage: Handbag containing silver spoon, cheque book, pen (**Mrs Grimley-Cloned**)
                Wheelchair with hardboard panels on sides and back, displaying "Dupo" in large letters, with red blanket (**Ted**)
                Crutches (**Bountiful**)

Personal: **Boxclever:** plastic spoon, cheque, small note book, pen
                Glow: false beard
                Bountiful: handkerchief (worn throughout)

ACT II

SCENE 1

Set: Clothes brush on desk
                Gallon jar of green jollop
                Small medicine bottle
                Bandages in cupboard
                Key in dispensary door lock

Off stage: Wheelchair with 2 microphones under cushion, blanket (**Ted**)
                Glass necklace (**Rosebud**)
                Handbag containing cheque book, pen (**Mrs Grimley-Cloned**)

Personal: **Bountiful:** plain cap

SCENE 2

On stage: As before

Off stage: Baby doll (**Mrs Spout**)
                Large bundle of forms (**Widdell**)

LIGHTING PLOT

Property fittings required: nil
1 interior. The same throughout

ACT I, Scene 1

To open: Lights up on empty waiting-room area

Cue 1   **Mrs Grimley-Cloned**: "I do not make mistakes."   (Page 2)
         Cross-fade to surgery

Cue 2   **Bountiful** goes off to change   (Page 5)
         Cross-fade to waiting-room

Cue 3   All stare at **Mrs Spout**   (Page 5)
         Bring up lights on surgery

Cue 4   **Mrs Spout**: "She should go to Harvey Street."   (Page 6)
         Fade lights down on waiting-room

Cue 5   **Boxclever** goes into dispensary   (Page 8)
         Bring up lights on dispensary

Cue 6   **Boxclever** and **Mrs Grimley-Cloned** go to waiting-room (Page 9)
         Cross-fade to waiting-room

Cue 7   **Ted** follows **Boxclever**   (Page 10)
         Cross-fade to surgery

Cue 8   **Mrs Spout** goes into waiting-room   (Page 13)
         Bring up lights on waiting-room

Cue 9   **Mrs Spout**: "…that's the trouble."   (Page 13)
         Fade lights down on waiting-room

Cue 10   **Bountiful** goes into waiting-room   (Page 14)
         Bring up lights on waiting-room

Cue 22   **Boxclever** follows **Glow** into surgery   (Page 37)
            Cross-fade to surgery

Cue 23   **Ted**: "Ted Rooter, investigative journalist."   (Page 41)
            Black-out

ACT II, SCENE 2

To open: Overall general lighting

No cues

EFFECTS PLOT

ACT I

Cue 1   Three **Workmen** enter   (Page 3)
Music, cut when ready

Cue 2   **Rosebud** and **Glow** look at each other   (Page 16)
Heavenly voices and twang of two arrows striking

Cue 3   **Rosebud** and **Glow** kiss   (Page 18)
Doorbell rings off L

Cue 4   **Glow** works on form   (Page 20)
Kaleidoscope of voices on tape as script page 20

Cue 5   **Boxclever**: "…if you'd like to——"   (Page 22)
*Heavenly choir followed by **Rosebud**'s voice on tape
as script page 22*

Cue 6   **Boxclever**: "…to some charity if you must."   (Page 23)
Rosebud's *voice on tape as script page 23*

Cue 7   **Boxclever**: "…surplus to where it is really needed."   (Page 27)
*Heavenly voices and **Rosebud**'s voice on tape as script
page 27*

ACT II

Cue 8   **Bountiful**: "…you haven't kissed the baby."   (Page 51)
Phone rings